TANI'S NEW HOME

Illustrated by Courtney Dawson

Library of Congress Cataloging-in-Publication Data

Names: Adewumi, Tani, 2010- author. | Dawson, Courtney, illustrator.

Title: Tani's new home: a refugee finds hope and kindness in America / Tanitoluwa Adewumi; with Michelle Lord; illustrated by Courtney Dawson.

Description: Nashville, TN: Thomas Nelson, 2020. | Audience: Ages 5-9 |

Summary: "The incredible true story of Tani Adewumi, a Nigerian refugee who garnered international news coverage after winning the New York State Chess Championship at the age of eight. Tani's story of finding a new life in America reminds children that perseverance and hope make a difference--and small acts of kindness can make the world a better place"-- Provided by publisher.

Identifiers: LCCN 2020021812 (print) | LCCN 2020021813 (ebook) | ISBN 9781400218288 (hardcover) | ISBN 9781400218332 (epub)

Subjects: LCSH: Adewumi, Tani, 2010---Juvenile literature. | Chess players--United States--Biography--Juvenile literature. | Refugees--United States--Biography--Juvenile literature. | Nigerian Americans--Biography--Juvenile literature. | Determination (Personality trait)--Juvenile literature. | Kindness--Juvenile literature. | Christian biography--Juvenile literature.

Classification: LCC GV1439.A34 A3 2020b (print) | LCC GV1439.A34 (ebook) | DDC 794.1092 [B]--dc23

LC record available at https://lccn.loc.gov/2020021812

LC ebook record available at https://lccn.loc.gov/2020021813

Printed in China

20 21 22 23 24 DSC 10 9 8 7 6 5 4 3 2 1

Mfr: DSC / Dongguan, China / October 2020 / PO# 9589870

TANI'S NEW HOME

A Refugee
Finds Hope
& Kindness
in America

TANITOLUWA ADEWUMI

illustrated by Courtney Dawson

Tommy
NELSON®

An Imprint of Thomas Nelson

In a home that felt as secure as a castle, in a fine neighborhood in Nigeria, Tani Adewumi lived with Dad, Mom, and his big brother, Austin. Their home was usually quiet and calm . . . until grandparents and aunts and uncles and cousins crowded inside.

Tani gobbled pounded yam and glugged egusi soup.

His great-uncles tapped the udu drums. *TUM-TUM, TUM.*

Mom and her sisters danced until the street vendors called,

"E kaaro.
Good morning."

One day, Dad returned home early from his print shop. His hands trembled.

"What is it?" Mom asked.

Some men from a terrorist group called Boko Haram had ordered Dad to print posters with messages of hate.

Dad had snuck away from his shop, but now the whole family was in danger.

Boko Haram hurt people who disagreed with them.

Tani's family packed everything, and Dad sped across Nigeria. Six hours later, he steered through an opening in a tall wall. Tani peered at the unfamiliar house.

Dad bolted the door.

Mom yanked the curtains closed.

But Austin made Tani feel safe. "I've got a great game," Austin said. **"Chess."** He sketched lines on a sheet of paper. "Color every other square." Tani worked his crayon side to side as Austin scissored another page into pieces.

Then they moved the paper pieces across the homemade board.

Tani didn't understand the rules, but he liked taking turns.

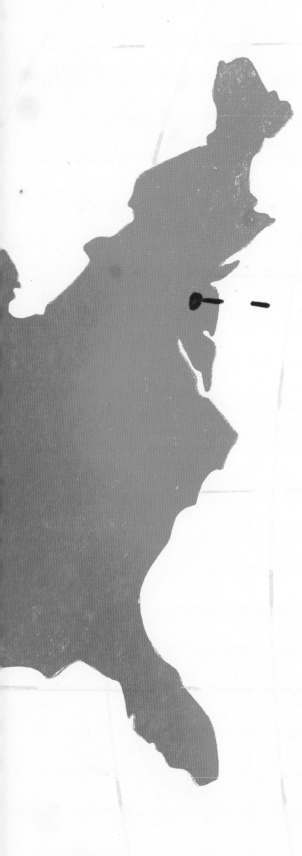

One morning, Tani awoke to see a chair wedged against the front door. Marks in the wooden door. Cracks in its frame. Boko Haram had found them. They had tried to break in.

"We are going to America," said Dad.

Tani's heart thrummed like an udu drum. **_TUM-TUM, TUM._**

"What does America look like?"

"You'll see," said Dad.

A few days later, Tani climbed into a real airplane! They flew for _hours_, slipping farther and farther from home.

At long last, they boarded a bus to New York City. Tani's eyes widened. The city shone as bright as day all through the night!

In Nigeria, lights sometimes went dark for weeks.

"Wow."

In a brick building, Mom and Dad filled out piles of paperwork for a place to live. Tani dozed on a bench. When Mom finally shook him awake, Tani bounded onto a bus that took them to a homeless shelter.

They stared up at the building. **"Thank You, God!"**

Tani smiled ear to ear. Until . . .

He saw their new place.

His parents lived in a teeny room on the fourth floor.

Tani and Austin lived in a teeny room on the fifth floor.

Two narrow beds. A dresser. A window. "This is a room, not a home," Tani said.

Outside cars **BEEPED** and **SCREECHED**. Someone screamed.

The city sounds were the same in Nigeria. Still, he wished his parents were down the hall as they'd always been.

Tani started a new school that had a number instead of a name: PS 116.

New faces surrounded him.

Most kids smiled.

Some whispered.

Finally, the bell rang for lunch. Tani's stomach growled. He craved the sting of habanero pepper on his tongue and the spicy steam of jollof rice in his nose. Instead, gooey stuff called *cheese* covered everything. **Cheese**burgers. **Cheese** pizza. Macaroni and **cheese**. *Ick.*

Then Tani went to a new kind of class—**chess**! But this chess was nothing like Austin's game.

Tani learned how **pawns**, **rooks**, and **knights** move.

He learned that the **queen** is the most powerful piece.

Tani imagined capturing another player's **king** to win a game.

Coach Shawn said, "Sometimes neither player can win. A tie in chess is called a *draw*."

After school, Tani raced to ask if he could join the chess club.

Mom stared at the sidewalk. The cost was too much.

"But . . . " Mom said. "Let me see what I can do."

One day, Mom burst into Tani's room. **"You can join the chess club!"**

"We can't afford it," he said.

Mom explained that she had emailed Coach Russ, who ran the club. She told Coach Russ that they lived in a shelter. "We don't have to pay anything."

Tani bounced into Mom's arms. "Thanks!"

In chess club, Coach Russ said, "The people who do the best in chess are the ones who work the hardest." Tani nodded. Chess wasn't about where you lived or what you owned. Chess was about hard work. **Tani was hooked!**

He taught Austin to play the *right* way. They practiced each day, and their room felt a little less cramped.

Weeks later, Tani played in his first tournament. He drew the first two games and lost the third. He scored the lowest out of *all* the players.

Chess was hard.

The next day, Tani remembered Coach Russ's words: *The people who do the best in chess are the ones who work the hardest.*

He sat at the front in chess club. He studied famous players. He played hundreds of chess puzzles. He challenged *everyone* to a match.

Tani competed in more tournaments—he even won some. His score climbed **higher** and **higher**.

One year later, Tani qualified for the state championship. Six matches. Two days. The very best chess players in New York!

ZIP. Tani whooshed his rook across the board and smacked the clock to stop the timer. **ZING!**

Suddenly, his challenger swiped his knight.

Tani gulped. **_Do. Not. Rush._** He made his face a calm mask. He would play like a king—one move at a time.

Finally, Tani won the game. Then he won the second game. And the third.

The next afternoon, while Tani waited for his last game, he heard someone say, "All Tani needs to do is draw." He had already scored more points than his next opponent. If they drew, they would each get half a point. Tani would be the champion!

His heart pounded like one thousand udu drums. **_TUM-TUM, TUM. TUM-TUM, TUM._**

Pieces battled on the board.

Rook forward.
Pawn captured pawn.
Knight up and over.
Rook to the side.

Tani sat tall. *I'm going to win.*
He concentrated. Hard.

His brain ached.

Then.

He.

Blundered.

His mistake gave the other
player a chance to win! Unless . . .

Tani gazed into his opponent's eyes. "I offer a draw." Would the
kid accept?

Tani's insides quivered as the clock *tick,*

tick,

ticked . . .

At last, his opponent nodded.

Coach Russ swung
Tani into the air.

**"You're the New
York state champion!"**

Teammates high-fived him.

"I'm so proud," Mom said.

A reporter heard about Tani. Headlines cheered:

This 8-Year-Old
Chess Champion Will
Make You Smile

A Homeless 8-Year-Old
Is Now a New York
Chess Champion

People around the world reached out to Tani and his family. They wanted to help. A stranger donated a car. Another gave Tani's family a surprise—an apartment of their own!

Although the apartment was mostly bare, Mom and Dad invited everyone over for a Nigerian feast. These friends weren't grandparents or aunts or uncles or cousins. But they were family all the same.

Tani scampered around the rooms.

"I have a home!"

MORE ABOUT TANI

Tanitoluwa Adewumi (*Tan-ee-tow-OO-ah Ad-eh-woom-ee*) was six years old when he left Nigeria. He and his family are refugees, people forced to flee their home country for fear of being harmed.

Since 2009, a group of terrorists called Boko Haram have spread through Nigeria like a terrible disease. They often attack Christians and bomb churches and schools. Throughout Nigeria, masked guards frisk families as they enter church. At stores, guards search shopping carts for bombs. Tani and Austin got used to soldiers with machine guns protecting their school. Boko Haram targeted Tani's family because of their Christian beliefs.

When the Adewumis were given a place to live in the New York City homeless shelter, Tani's dad said, "Let us show our appreciation for this blessing by being a blessing to others." This message stuck with Tani.

After eight-year-old Tani became the New York state chess champion, an article about him appeared in *The New York Times*. His story touched people. Coach Russ set up a GoFundMe account to collect money for the Adewumis so they could pay for a home. People around the world wanted to help. Many sent $5 or $10. Some people gave more. One stranger gave Tani's family a place to live—an apartment of their own. Tani has learned that with God, "anything is possible."

Remembering what his dad taught him about being a blessing to others, Tani said, "I want to help other kids." Incredibly, Tani and his family donated *all* of the money to help children in need learn to play chess!